953
Sa

Saudi Arabia in
pictures

DATE DUE

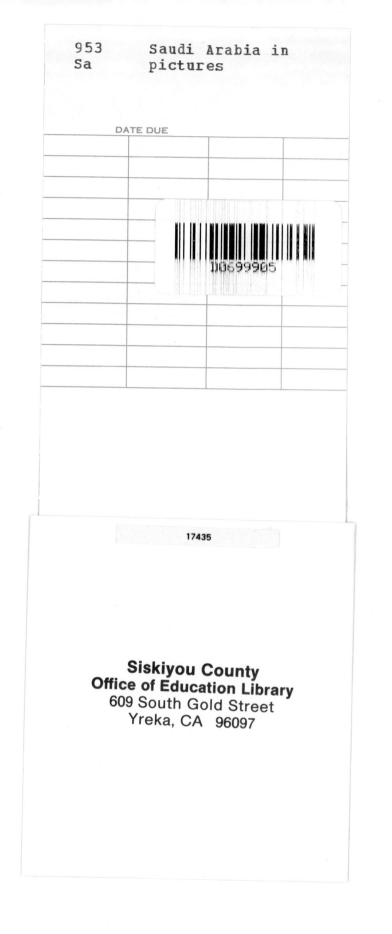

# SAUDI ARABIA
## ...in Pictures

Visual Geography Series®

# SAUDI ARABIA

## ...in Pictures

Prepared by
**Geography Department**

**Lerner Publications Company**
Minneapolis

Courtesy of F. Mattioli/FAO

**A Saudi worker plants seeds by hand on an experimental farm in Saudi Arabia.**

This is an all-new edition of the Visual Geography Series. Previous editions have been published by Sterling Publishing Company, New York City, and some of the original textual information has been retained. New photographs, maps, charts, captions, and updated information have been added. The text has been entirely reset in 10/12 Century Textbook.

LIBRARY OF CONGRESS CATALOGING-IN-PUBLICATION DATA

Saudi Arabia in pictures.
  (Visual geography series)
  Rev. ed. of: Saudi Arabia in pictures / prepared by Eugene Gordon.
  Includes index.
  Summary: Introduces the geography, history, economy, culture, and people of the large middle eastern country that occupies most of the Arabian Peninsula.
  1. Saudi Arabia. I. Gordon, Eugene, 1923- . Saudi Arabia in pictures.  II. Lerner Publications Company. Geography Dept.  III. Series: Visual geography series (Minneapolis, Minn.)
  DS204.S313   1989      953'.8            88–7335
  ISBN 0-8225-1845-7

International Standard Book Number: 0-8225-1845-7
Library of Congress Catalog Card Number: 88-7335

## VISUAL GEOGRAPHY SERIES®

**Publisher**
Harry Jonas Lerner
**Associate Publisher**
Nancy M. Campbell
**Senior Editor**
Mary M. Rodgers
**Editor**
Gretchen Bratvold
**Assistant Editors**
Dan Filbin
Kathleen S. Heidel
**Illustrations Editor**
Karen A. Sirvaitis
**Consultants/Contributors**
Dr. Ruth F. Hale
Isaac Eshel
Sandra K. Davis
**Designer**
Jim Simondet
**Cartographer**
Carol F. Barrett
**Indexer**
Sylvia Timian
**Production Manager**
Richard J. Hannah

Independent Picture Service

**Muslims (followers of the Islamic religion) gather in tents at one of the stops on their religious journey in Saudi Arabia.**

**Acknowledgments**

Title page photo courtesy of S. M. Amin/*Aramco World.*

Elevation contours adapted from *The Times Atlas of the World,* seventh comprehensive edition (New York: Times Books, 1985).

1  2  3  4  5  6  7  8  9  10  98  97  96  95  94  93  92  91  90  89

Courtesy of Royal Commission of Jubail and Yanbu

Students compete in a race under their teacher's guidance. This modern track is one of many new sports complexes that have been built during the 1970s and 1980s in Saudi Arabia.

# Contents

**Introduction** . . . . . . . . . . . . . . . . . . . . . . . . . . . . . . . . . . . . . . . . . . . . . . . . . **7**

**1) The Land** . . . . . . . . . . . . . . . . . . . . . . . . . . . . . . . . . . . . . . . . . . . . . . . . **9**
Topography. The Oases. Climate. Flora. Fauna. Natural Resources. Cities.

**2) History and Government** . . . . . . . . . . . . . . . . . . . . . . . . . . . . . . . . . . . . **23**
Ancient History. The Growth of Trade. The Birth of Islam. Arab Conquests and Disunity. The Wahhabis and the Saud Dynasty. Origins of a Nation. Oil Transforms the Desert. The Oil Embargo. Recent Events. Government.

**3) The People** . . . . . . . . . . . . . . . . . . . . . . . . . . . . . . . . . . . . . . . . . . . . . . . **38**
Nomadic and Village Life. Urban Life. Religion. Education and Language. Health. The Arts and Communications. Marriage, Social Life, and Customs. Food and Recreation.

**4) The Economy** . . . . . . . . . . . . . . . . . . . . . . . . . . . . . . . . . . . . . . . . . . . . . **52**
The Oil Industry. Agriculture and Industry. Transportation. Water and Energy. The Future.

**Index** . . . . . . . . . . . . . . . . . . . . . . . . . . . . . . . . . . . . . . . . . . . . . . . . . . . . . **64**

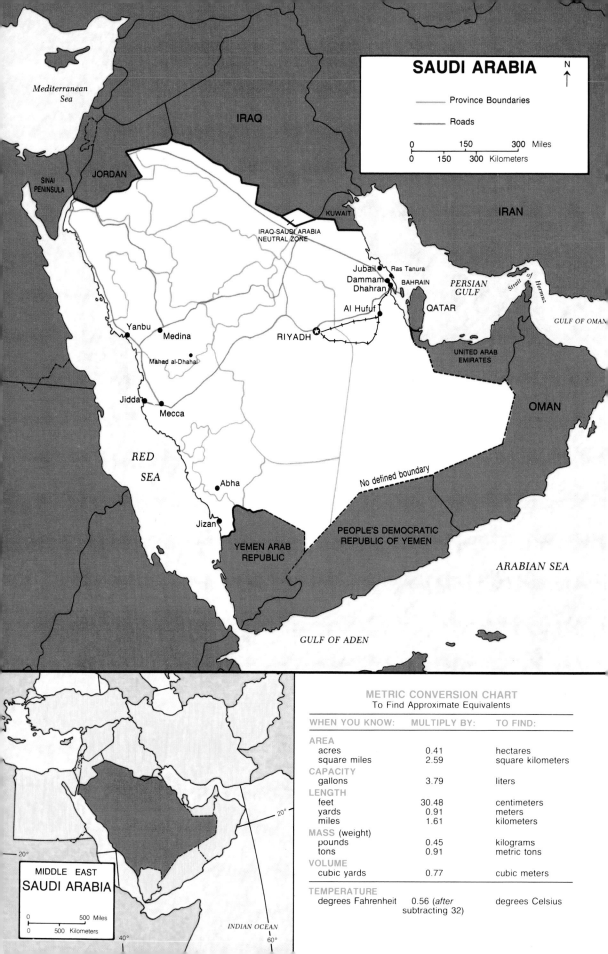

## SAUDI ARABIA

N

— Province Boundaries
— Roads

| 0 | 150 | 300 | Miles |
| 0 | 150 | 300 | Kilometers |

*Mediterranean Sea*

IRAQ

JORDAN

SINAI PENINSULA

KUWAIT

IRAQ-SAUDI ARABIA NEUTRAL ZONE

IRAN

Jubail • Ras Tanura
Dammam
Dhahran • BAHRAIN

*PERSIAN GULF*

QATAR

*Strait of Hormuz*

GULF OF OMAN

Al Hufuf

RIYADH

UNITED ARAB EMIRATES

Yanbu
Medina

Mahad al-Dhahal •

OMAN

Jidda
Mecca

*RED SEA*

Abha

No defined boundary

Jizan

PEOPLE'S DEMOCRATIC REPUBLIC OF YEMEN

*ARABIAN SEA*

YEMEN ARAB REPUBLIC

*GULF OF ADEN*

MIDDLE EAST
**SAUDI ARABIA**

20°

20°

40°

60°

INDIAN OCEAN

| 0 | 500 | Miles |
| 0 | 500 | Kilometers |

## METRIC CONVERSION CHART
To Find Approximate Equivalents

| WHEN YOU KNOW: | MULTIPLY BY: | TO FIND: |
|---|---|---|
| **AREA** | | |
| acres | 0.41 | hectares |
| square miles | 2.59 | square kilometers |
| **CAPACITY** | | |
| gallons | 3.79 | liters |
| **LENGTH** | | |
| feet | 30.48 | centimeters |
| yards | 0.91 | meters |
| miles | 1.61 | kilometers |
| **MASS** (weight) | | |
| pounds | 0.45 | kilograms |
| tons | 0.91 | metric tons |
| **VOLUME** | | |
| cubic yards | 0.77 | cubic meters |
| **TEMPERATURE** | | |
| degrees Fahrenheit | 0.56 (*after* subtracting 32) | degrees Celsius |

Saudi Arabia has many square miles of desert territory. The sand dunes of the Rub al-Khali region are uninhabited, but geologists are testing the area for underground oil deposits like those found in other parts of the country.

# Introduction

The Kingdom of Saudi Arabia occupies 80 percent of the Arabian Peninsula. Although it is a very large country, much of Saudi Arabia is inhospitable desert with little or no rainfall. The land contains no rivers or lakes, and daytime temperatures can reach 130° F before giving way to the chill of night.

The discovery of oil in the late 1930s changed life in this desert country. Until about 1940 Saudi Arabia remained much as it had been for hundreds of years. With the revenue that oil produces, however, Saudi Arabia has become a powerful and active member in the community of Middle Eastern nations. One of the charter members of the Arab League—an organization founded in 1945 to promote closer ties among Arab countries—Saudi Arabia has often been a leader in the league's council meetings.

To gain better control of its rapidly growing petroleum industry, Saudi Arabia joined with the South American country

The main entrance to Al-Haram, the central place of worship in Mecca, was first built in the eighth century A.D. Since then it has been continually repaired and enlarged.

prices and oil production quotas beneficial to its members, and Saudi Arabia plays a pivotal role in OPEC's often difficult policy negotiations.

In the 1980s the war between Iran and Iraq began to threaten the stability of the Arab region, particularly the transportation of oil to world markets. Because oil is its chief source of income, Saudi Arabia depends on shipping lanes in the Persian Gulf remaining open and safe for oil tankers. As a result, King Fahd of Saudi Arabia strongly supported the United Nations (UN) cease-fire agreement that went into effect in August 1988.

Saudi Arabia's oil wealth propelled it into the industrial world, and its swift economic growth created many contrasts. Modern concrete and steel buildings stand near adobe houses, and cars and donkeys jostle for position on newly built roads. Muezzins (criers), who call Muslims (followers of Islam) to prayer, blend with radios that play hit songs from Cairo, Egypt. Amid all these contrasts, Saudi Arabia works to develop a modern yet traditionally Islamic nation in which its citizens can benefit from the sale of its oil.

of Venezuela in 1960 to invite other oil-producing nations to form the Organization of Petroleum Exporting Countries (OPEC). This group works to establish oil

A Saudi Arabian technician adjusts a valve on an oil rig against the backdrop of a mosque (Islamic place of worship) used by Muslim oil workers.

Jagged peaks are typical of the mountains of the Asir region. At high elevations only shrubs and small trees grow on the rocky slopes.

# 1) The Land

Saudi Arabia contains approximately 860,000 square miles of territory—about the size of the United States from the East Coast to the Mississippi River. The Red Sea marks Saudi Arabia's western border, and Jordan, Iraq, and Kuwait lie to the north. To the east are the Persian Gulf, the nation of Qatar, and the United Arab Emirates. The Yemen Arab Republic, the People's Democratic Republic of Yemen, and Oman form Saudi Arabia's southern frontier. Many of these international boundaries are not clearly defined, particularly along the southern line.

## Topography

The Arabian Peninsula, which is composed mostly of Saudi Arabia, slopes downward from the west to the east. The region has mountains on its western edge, large areas of desert, and no permanent aboveground supplies of water. Saudi Arabia can be divided into six main geographical areas: Hejaz, Asir, Nejd, Al-Nafud, Rub al-Khali, and Al-Hasa.

The mountainous west coast of Saudi Arabia is made up of the Hejaz region in the north and of the Asir region in the south. In Hejaz, the mountains average

9

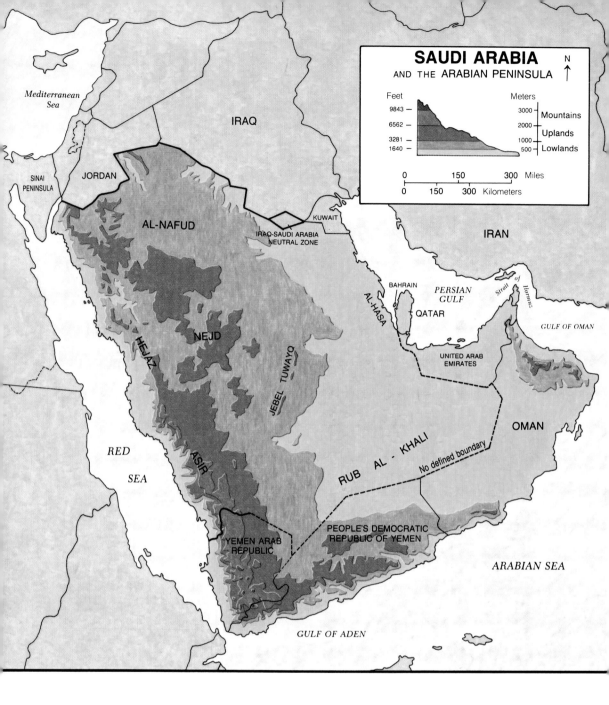

almost 7,000 feet above sea level and often drop abruptly into the sea, leaving very little area of coastal plain and very few navigable harbors. Most settlements lie on the more gently sloping eastern side of the mountains, where oases—watered areas—are located.

A gap in the mountains near the city of Mecca interrupts the coastal range and marks the end of Hejaz and the beginning of the Asir region. The coastal plain is broader in this southern region, sometimes reaching almost 40 miles in width, and the mountains are generally higher than those in Hejaz. Asir is the most fertile region in Saudi Arabia. Farmers cultivate its coastal strip and carve terraces into its mountains to create level farmland.

The mountains of Hejaz and Asir taper off to the east into large, irregular plateaus. This rocky area—called Nejd—occupies central Saudi Arabia and contains a few small deserts and some isolated mountains. Wadis—dry riverbeds that carry water from brief seasonal rains—run eastward toward the Persian Gulf. In the middle of Nejd lies the Jebel Tuwayq, a long series of ridges that rise from 300 to 900 feet above the plateau.

North of Nejd is the desert region of Al-Nafud, with sand dunes that extend for miles. The sand contains a high level of iron oxide, which often gives it a red tint. Very few oases exist in this desert, and very little rain falls. When winter rains come, scrub grasses grow for a brief period. Nomadic herders bring their flocks to feed on the short-lived plants in early spring.

To the south of Nejd lies the huge Rub al-Khali, or Empty Quarter. The largest sand desert in the world, this region is nearly uninhabited, and years may pass before rain falls. Approximately 250,000 square miles in area, Rub al-Khali is almost as big as the state of Texas.

In the east, along the Persian Gulf, lies the coastal plain of Al-Hasa. Made up of sand and gravel plains, Al-Hasa—the source of Saudi Arabia's vast oil wealth—holds the largest known deposits of petroleum in the world.

Farmers terrace the hills of Asir, taking full advantage of every acre of the area's fertile soil.

Underground water supplies feed large oases (fertile areas), which sustain communities of up to several thousand people. Small oases cannot support permanent residents and are useful only as rest stops for travelers.

Herders have allowed these camels to rest as they travel through the Al-Hasa region. This area of the country yields an abundance of oil.

## The Oases

Except for wadis, which contain water only during the rainy season, Saudi Arabia does not have any rivers or lakes. Other waterways include the small canals dug next to wells that transport water to the fields. The country gets its water primarily from underground sources.

An oasis is often an island of greenery in an otherwise barren desert. Its fertility is caused by underground springs or wells, and the amount of water that is available determines the size of the oasis. Some oases consist of a few palm trees around a muddy water hole and support only temporary inhabitants. Other oases cover a number of square miles and enable a permanent population of several thousand people to live nearby. Oasis dwellers raise camels, sheep, and goats and grow a variety of vegetables and fruits.

In places where the water supply is sufficient to last an entire year, large-scale agriculture takes place. Rainwater, which is quickly absorbed by the sand and gravel, feeds some wells. Other wells are maintained by underground supplies that were formed millions of years ago. By digging more wells and by setting up irrigation systems, the Saudi government has created many artificial oases. These areas make it possible for people to settle permanently in the desert and to grow their own food.

## Climate

Saudi Arabia has a very dry, hot climate with frequent dust and sand storms. Summer temperatures can rise to 130° F during the day, dropping to about 40° to 50° F at night. Temperatures along the coasts of the Red Sea and the Persian Gulf are not as uncomfortable, but the humidity is much higher, particularly near the Persian Gulf, which is known for its frequent, heavy fogs.

In the central and northern parts of the country, temperatures seldom drop below

A young Saudi Arabian carries dates that have been harvested from one of the oases in Hejaz.

freezing in the winter. Riyadh, Saudi Arabia's capital city, is cool in the winter, with daytime temperatures dropping as low as 50° F. In July the temperature averages 93° F.

The average annual rainfall for the country is four inches. Often an entire year's

Rain quickly saturates the desert soil and just as quickly evaporates, causing the land to crack in some areas of the country.

rain comes in one or two downpours between October and March. The Asir region receives the most rain—12 to 20 inches—while some areas, such as the Rub al-Khali, receive no rain for many years in a row.

## Flora

Vegetation in Saudi Arabia is generally sparse because of lack of rain and poor soil. Trees are a rare sight and are completely absent in most areas. The country's only forests are made up of wild olive and juniper trees, which grow in the mountains of the Asir region. Small shrubs and herbs—especially plants of the mustard and chamomile families—are common. Most plants have adapted to the conditions of desert existence, some by reducing their leaf surface area. For example, plants with spiny or needlelike leaves lose less water from evaporation. Other plants have the ability to store water, and some are even able to take nourishment from salt water.

Among small trees and shrubs that have adapted to the desert climate are the aloe plant and the tamarisk tree, both of which are found in much of the country. At high altitudes, fig trees and carob trees (an evergreen with red flowers) flourish, as well as cactuslike euphorbias.

Wildflowers are abundant at high elevations, particularly during the rainy season. Reeds provide material for building small dwellings and for thatching roofs. In the deserts, widely scattered shrubs grow, especially the *hadh*, a kind of saltbush.

## Fauna

Small, swift gazelles and large-horned oryx (a type of antelope) once roamed freely in Saudi Arabia, but now they are rarely seen. Meat eaters—such as wolves, hyenas, and jackals—can be found, and smaller mammals include foxes, ratels (badgerlike animals), rabbits, hedgehogs, and jerboas (rodents with long hind legs). Ibex (wild goats) live in the mountains of the Hejaz region, and baboons populate the highlands of Asir.

The most important animal in the history of Saudi Arabia is the camel. This animal made travel possible in the barren and frequently waterless desert. The camel of Arabia—the dromedary—has a single hump and flat, thick-soled hooves that do not sink in sand. Because camels have the ability to go without water for several days—and longer if they find juicy plants to eat—they are especially adapted to desert life.

Evidence suggests that horses have lived in the Arabian Peninsula for nearly 3,000 years and have been tamed for the last 1,500 years. In Saudi Arabia, a distinctive breed developed—the small Arabian horse, which has great stamina and speed and which is an ancestor of the thoroughbred horse known in Western nations. Horses, like camels, have played a very important

Courtesy of Royal Commission of Jubail and Yanbu

Sculptured gardens grace the landscape in the city of Yanbu.

Independent Picture Service

Southwest Asia (including Saudi Arabia) and North Africa have at times been struck by hordes of desert locusts that eat all the vegetation in their path. The last plague, consisting of billions of the insects, began in the 1950s and lasted for several years. In the late 1980s another plague threatened the region.

Independent Picture Service

Arabian horses are prized not only in Saudi Arabia but throughout the world.

part in the history of Arabia. Although horses lack the endurance of camels and have never been used for long desert journeys, throughout the ages they have provided speedy transportation for Arab warriors.

Locusts (grasshoppers) have a history of bringing devastation to Saudi crops. Some of the nomads of Saudi Arabia eat locusts. Many other species of insects, as well as snakes, lizards, and scorpions, are native to the Arabian Peninsula. The coastal wa-

Independent Picture Service

Egrets are among the birds that visit the western shore of the Arabian Peninsula as they migrate between Europe and Africa.

Courtesy of Royal Embassy of Saudi Arabia

Along with many other species, angelfish thrive in the Red Sea.

ters contain many varieties of fish, especially in the coral reefs of the Red Sea.

Although ostriches are now extinct in Saudi Arabia, flamingos, egrets, pelicans, and many other shorebirds are still common. The nation's birdlife is migratory— that is, it visits the country during fall and spring as the various species fly between Europe and Africa. The most common bird in the oases is the bulbul, a songbird that appears often in the popular poetry of the country. Eagles, vultures, and owls are also frequently seen.

**15**

## Natural Resources

Saudi Arabia's most profitable natural resource is its vast petroleum deposits. Hundreds of millions of years ago the waters of the Persian Gulf covered much of eastern and northern Saudi Arabia, as well as Kuwait and parts of Iran. During the time that this land was under water, vast quantities of dead plants and animals came to rest on the sea floor. Eventually the land rose, the gulf shrank, and large areas that had been submerged became dry. The pressure of the earth slowly changed the natural deposits into oil. The gulf area now contains more than 25 percent of the world's known oil reserves.

As a result of the abundance of oil, the Saudis have developed several other related products—petrochemicals, fertilizers, and liquid propane gas. Besides oil, the

Courtesy of Bechtel Company

Some of Saudi Arabia's oil comes from rigs drilled into the floor of the Persian Gulf. The petroleum is piped ashore from drilling platforms.

Independent Picture Service

Petroleum geologists probe the Rub al-Khali (the Empty Quarter) for oil.

16

**At a project site that is located 35 miles north of Riyadh, 160 solar panels harness the sun's power in the world's largest installation for gathering solar energy.**

most commonly found minerals in Saudi Arabia are gold, silver, and copper. Bauxite (from which aluminum is made) ranks second to petroleum in volume. Other minerals—including zinc, nickel, pyrite (used in making sulfur), molybdenum (an element used to strengthen steel), phosphate, gypsum (a mineral used in making plaster), magnesite, and salt—have been found. Recently the Saudis have reopened the ancient gold mines at Mahad al-Dhahal and at Al-Masane.

**As it searches for the land's mineral wealth, the Saudi government sponsors exploratory mining operations.**

Merchants in a shop in Dammam, a city on the Persian Gulf, admire finely crafted gold pieces and debate the purchase price.

## Cities

Although many of its people have traditionally been nomads and village dwellers, Saudi Arabia's cities are growing quickly. The success of the nation's petroleum sales has resulted in the development of processing facilities, management and business centers, and workers' housing projects. Not all Saudi cities are new, however, and the country's ancient Arab culture has strongly influenced its long-established cities.

### CAPITAL CITIES

Riyadh—the political and administrative capital of the country—is located in an oasis in the Nejd region. Oil wealth has enabled planners to guide the city's development. Spacious roadways and modern, steel-and-glass buildings now dominate the capital, and the population has risen from 8,000 residents at the beginning of the twentieth century to over 1.8 million in the late 1980s. In addition to being the business headquarters for the oil industry, Riyadh is also prominent in the manufacture of cement, plastics, and prefabricated houses.

Mecca, the religious capital of the country and the most sacred city for Muslims throughout the world, is the birthplace of the Islamic prophet Muhammad. Situated in a rocky valley of southern Hejaz, Mecca has a population of about 500,000 people. Due to the hot, dry climate of the area, few farms exist near the city, and, except for the manufacture of religious articles, there is little local industry. In ancient

Riyadh is the center of political and economic activity in the nation. The traditional home of the Saud clan, Riyadh has experienced immense growth in the twentieth century.

Al-Haram, the grand mosque at Mecca, dominates the city of Muhammad's birth. Its tall minarets (towers) offer muezzin (criers) the opportunity to call faithful Muslims to prayer.

**19**

Originally constructed in the eighth century, Al-Haram has grown larger and more ornate over the centuries.

times, Mecca was located at the cross-roads of caravan routes, making it an important market town. Today Mecca's wealth depends on the visits of religious pilgrims from all over the world. Several million Muslims make the journey each year, and the challenge of housing and feeding them is enormous.

### SECONDARY CITIES

Saudi Arabia's second most important sacred city is Medina, to which Muham-

Islam prohibits representations of the human form. A page of the Koran is decorated along its borders with floral and geometric designs.

mad fled in A.D. 622 when the residents of Mecca grew hostile toward him. Medina has 290,000 people and is located at an oasis that produces dates, other fruits, and grains. Medina is the site of the Islamic University, which is an important school for Islamic studies. Nearby is the Medina Library, which contains Arabic texts on religion, geography, and medicine. The most valuable book in this institution is an edition of the Koran (the Islamic book of holy writings). It is handwritten on parchment and dates from the seventh century A.D.—when the religion of Islam began.

Medina, which means "city of the prophet," is another stop on a Muslim's religious journey. This open-air suq (market) sells many of the food products that come from desert oases as well as handcrafted religious mementos. Muslims from many nations mingle in the corridors of the suq as they do their shopping.

21

A traditional house in Jidda shows classic Arabic designs in its plaster facade, arched doorways, and windows.

Situated on the Red Sea in Hejaz, Jidda is one of the country's leading seaports. Its 750,000 inhabitants are of many ethnic backgrounds—Arab, Persian, African, and Indian. Rugs and religious articles are manufactured locally, but the biggest source of income comes from religious pilgrims. About 90 percent of all pilgrims traveling from foreign lands to Mecca enter Saudi Arabia through Jidda's port. Jidda has the country's largest bazaar (marketplace), which is filled with goods from both the eastern and the western worlds.

Headquarters of the Arabian American Oil Company (ARAMCO), Dhahran is an oil camp in the Al-Hasa region, where much of the country's oil exploration and processing takes place. The city has developed rapidly since the discovery of oil and features air-conditioned, prefabricated houses and supermarkets that contrast sharply with the surrounding desert.

Jidda is one of the few deepwater ports on the Red Sea. Modern technology has made loading and unloading goods in the dock area more efficient.

The Nabataeans, who controlled trade routes in the northwestern part of the country from 350 B.C. to A.D. 100, built the temples at Madayen Saleh into rock cliffs.

# 2) History and Government

The development of Islam in the seventh century A.D. was such a pivotal event in the history of Saudi Arabia that much of what happened before Muhammad's birth is unrecorded. Only since the 1960s have archaeological expeditions begun to explore the history of the Arabian Peninsula's early peoples.

## Ancient History

The earliest traces of the inhabitants of Saudi Arabia come from the coast of the Persian Gulf, near the city of Dhahran. Archaeologists have found evidence of a settled, agricultural people there dating from about 5000 B.C. The majority of the people in Saudi Arabia, however, are the descendants of nomads who lived near the oases and who roamed the deserts in search of grazing areas for their herds. These residents of the Arabian Peninsula spoke a Semitic language that eventually developed into modern Arabic.

Probably in search of food, many nomadic Arabs migrated to the regions northwest of Arabia. In about 3500 B.C. groups of Arabs settled in the Sinai Peninsula and in Egypt. Another migration of Arabs went northeastward into Babylonia (modern Iraq). Later, in about 2500 B.C. and again in 1500 B.C., waves of nomadic Arabs settled in the Fertile Crescent (a semicircle of land from the southeastern Mediterranean coast to the Persian Gulf).

The Dilmun civilization flourished along the coast of the Persian Gulf around 2000 B.C. The inhabitants of Dilmun traded with regions that are in present-day Iraq and India.

## The Growth of Trade

Many descendants of the Arab migrants returned to Arabia beginning around 1200 B.C. They became merchants and traded spices from India; ivory, animal skins, and slaves from Africa; and jewels, gold, and incense from Arabia itself. Starting from southern and western Arabia, a network of important caravan routes crossed the Arabian Peninsula to Egypt, Palestine (modern Israel), Syria, and Babylonia.

Early inhabitants of what is now Saudi Arabia transported precious commodities from the south to more densely settled

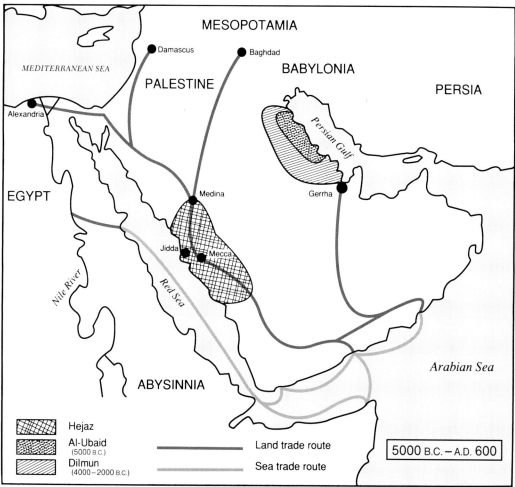

Artwork by Mindy A. Rabin

**Throughout its history Saudi Arabia has been a crossroads for trade routes. Over the centuries, traders passed through Hejaz on their way to the Mediterranean region and also came in contact with the Al-Ubiad and Dilmun civilizations on the Persian Gulf.**

Wind sculpts the sands of the desert into graceful dunes. People traveling with the trade caravans fought the dry winds and shifting sands to reach their destinations.

areas in the north and the west. These communities wanted the products that southern Arabia had to offer, as well as the goods that came from East Africa and India by overland routes and by sea.

The Sabaean people—traders from southeastern Saudi Arabia—prospered from the tenth century to the first century B.C. In about 350 B.C. the Nabataeans in northwestern Saudi Arabia and present-day Jordan gained control of some of the commercial routes. Because of difficult navigation in the northern half of the Red Sea, many ships stopped along the Arabian coast to unload goods for the caravan portion of the journey. Caravan cities like Jidda, Mecca, and Medina grew as trade centers and provided pack animals, food, and lodging. Camels, originally raised as dairy animals, became the most common means of transport.

Eventually, Egyptian, Greek, and Roman merchants cut into the Arab control of the sea routes, and Arab leadership in trade declined. Within Arabia, the kingdoms that controlled the caravan routes became less unified, with individual caravan cities and independent nomadic groups wielding more power. Arabia continued to be a commercial crossroads but secured fewer profits because of infighting among Arab tribes for control of the trade routes. In the mid-sixth century the Ethiopians controlled southern Arabia for a brief period, only to be replaced in A.D. 575 by the Persians (from present-day Iran).

The Quraysh people—fighters from the deserts of northern Arabia—gained control of Mecca by the beginning of the sixth century. The religious leader Muhammad was born to a family within this influential group in Mecca in A.D. 570.

**25**

Muslim artisans in many countries have applied their skill to making finely lettered copies of the Koran in Arabic. As the book of sacred Islamic writings, the Koran contains a record of the messages Muhammad received from God.

Courtesy of Cultural and Tourism Office of the Turkish Embassy

## The Birth of Islam

Until he reached the age of 40, Muhammad led the life of a well-to-do merchant. In about A.D. 610, however, this trader began to speak about visions he was receiving from God. According to these revelations, God chose him to teach the religion that came to be known as Islam. Muhammad's visions continued all his life and were eventually recorded in the Koran.

Meanwhile, Mecca continued to attract great numbers of worshipers who kept sacred statues of their gods in a holy place called the Kaaba. The merchants of Mecca viewed Muhammad with great suspicion because he preached the destruction of the statues and instead called for the worship of the single, invisible God called Allah. By A.D. 622 Muhammad had made many enemies, who forced him to flee to the city of Yathrib (soon to be called Medina, which means the "city of the prophet"). Muhammad's escape is called the Hegira, and this event in 622 marks the beginning of the Islamic calendar.

During the rest of his life Muhammad spread his influence and teachings over much of Arabia, and he and his followers engaged in an activity common to many Arab traders—caravan raiding. Muslim warriors soon gained great wealth and a warlike reputation. In 630 Muhammad returned to Mecca and occupied it easily. He soon destroyed the statues in the Kaaba and turned the site into a holy place for Islamic worship.

With the help of new Muslim converts from Mecca, Muhammad overcame the other peoples of the Hejaz region. Soon many more were eager to join the powerful and wealthy Muslims. Muhammad became the head of many of these groups, which he ruled from Mecca. By the time Muhammad died in 632, Hejaz, Nejd, and much of the southern and eastern Arabian Peninsula were Islamic.

## Arab Conquests and Disunity

In the century after Muhammad's death, Arabs began to travel to other regions under the banner of Islam. Islamic Arab warriors conquered Egypt, North Africa, and Spain to the west, and Syria, Meso-potamia (part of modern Iraq), Persia, Afghanistan, and parts of India and central Asia to the north and east.

During these Muslim conquests, Arabia itself began to decline in political importance. The Umayyad clan took over the caliphate (the Islamic religious leadership) in the late seventh century and moved the political center of Islam to Damascus, Syria. (The religious center of Islam remained at Mecca.) Consequently, direct ties between the Arabian Peninsula and conquered lands and cultures were greatly weakened. The Arab peoples in Arabia fell into political disorder and fought among themselves.

Through the centuries many unsuccessful attempts to unite or rule the various Arab groups occurred, but the Arabian Peninsula remained politically fragmented.

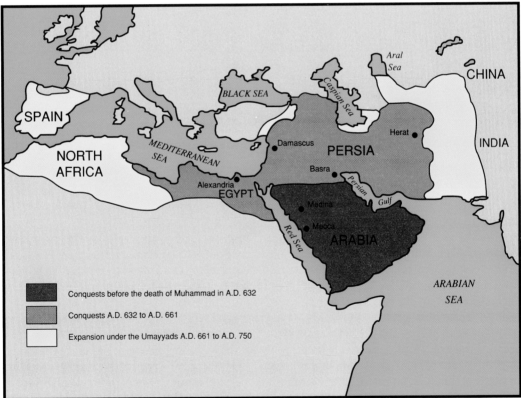

Artwork by Mindy A. Rabin

Beginning in Mecca and Medina, Muslim armies conquered much of the Arabian Peninsula before Muhammad's death in 632. In the next century Muslim victories extended Arab control northwest into Africa and Europe and east into Asia.

A pottery lamp of the kind used in mosques during the fourteenth century is decorated with floral and geometric designs, according to the Islamic custom of banning human representations.

In the mid-fifteenth century, however, the Saud clan moved into Nejd from Al-Hasa, started date plantations, and traded successfully along the caravan routes. The Sauds slowly increased their power throughout the region.

During the fifteenth century European merchants sought new markets, and for a brief time the Portuguese traded along the Hejaz coast of the Red Sea. Later, in the sixteenth and seventeenth centuries, Ottoman Turks conquered the Hejaz area of Saudi Arabia, as well as the regions of Egypt and Syria. The Ottomans maintained distant control of Arabia until the nineteenth century, allowing Arabian clans to rule locally.

## The Wahhabis and the Saud Dynasty

During the many centuries of Arab disunity, Islam was generally weak throughout Arabia. The Saud clan in Nejd, however, still followed the teachings of Islam. In the early eighteenth century, a Muslim named Abd al-Wahhab led an Islamic revival movement along with Muhammad ibn Saud, a member of the Saud family. The reform movement—called Wahhabism—was based on a literal interpretation of the Koran. Its sacred writings strictly limited the use of pictures in religious life and demanded the fulfillment of Islamic laws. The Saud and al-Wahhab families intermarried, strengthening their alliance. During the nineteenth century, these leaders and their descendants conquered most of Arabia, unifying the country and strengthening the practice of Islam.

As a result of Saudi territorial gains, the Sauds came into conflict with the Ottoman

This nineteenth-century drawing shows Mecca during the time the Saud and al-Wahhab families were leading a movement for the reformation of Islam.

A row of parading riders of the National Guard recall the time of Ibn Saud's victories, which unified the country in the early twentieth century.

Turks. In 1818 Turkish forces, which had seldom ventured into Arabia, invaded and occupied Nejd. The foreign troops were unable to maintain control over the desert fighters, however, and the Sauds reasserted their power in 1824. The Sauds established Riyadh as their capital city.

## Origins of a Nation

The modern history of Saudi Arabia began in 1902, when Abd al-Aziz al-Saud (also known as Ibn Saud) became head of the Saud clan. He and his followers consolidated Saud control of Arabia. By 1914 Ibn Saud had established full authority over the provinces of Nejd and Al-Hasa and was recognized as the leader of Nejd by the British during World War I (1914–1918). By the end of the war the Ottoman Empire—which had sided with Germany against Great Britain—completely lost its hold over its Middle Eastern territories.

The British were sympathetic to Ibn Saud because he had helped to push the Ottomans out of Arabia. Yet the British gave most of their support to Ibn Saud's rival, the emir (prince) Hussein, ruler of Hejaz. With the aid of the famous British soldier T. E. Lawrence (Lawrence of Arabia), Emir Hussein revolted against the Ottomans. Hussein then declared himself king of Hejaz. He ruled briefly, however, because Ibn Saud soon defeated him, and by 1925 Ibn Saud extended his own rule over Hejaz.

In 1926 Ibn Saud proclaimed himself king of Hejaz and sultan (ruler) of Nejd, and in 1932 the two areas were united into the Kingdom of Saudi Arabia. Through these actions, Ibn Saud began to dominate Arabian politics and ended the local fighting within the country. He established a firm, centralized rule, and, by strictly enforcing Islamic law, he gradually created a unified country.

Large supplies of petroleum have increased Saudi Arabia's economic vitality. Economic growth, in turn, has altered the nation's traditional social patterns.

## Oil Transforms the Desert

In 1933 Ibn Saud granted the right to explore for oil to ARAMCO. The company discovered Saudi Arabia's first important well in 1938, and major oil production started in 1946.

Within 25 years, the huge income from oil sales brought about many changes in Saudi Arabia. The country that had existed in isolation from the outside world suddenly had international systems of transportation and communication, with airports, television stations, and diesel-fueled trucks.

This rapid transformation took its toll on Arabian culture. Ibn Saud himself lived modestly, but government advisers often mismanaged the money that poured into the country. In 1953 Ibn Saud died at the age of 73, and his eldest son, Saud ibn Abd al-Aziz succeeded him.

King Saud proved to be a poor administrator and paid little attention to economic matters. By 1958 the government faced difficult financial conditions because of King Saud's policies. The Saudi royal family convinced King Saud to allow his younger but more experienced brother Faisal to run the government.

Faisal, who was born in 1906, had shown administrative ability from the time he was very young. In 1925 he had been appointed viceroy of Hejaz, and in 1930 he had been given the post of foreign minister, which enabled him to travel widely, visiting the United States, Spain, and many Arab countries. Between 1958 and 1964 Faisal consolidated his control of the country, and on November 2, 1964, the senior members of the royal family proclaimed him king. The former king, Saud, died in 1969.

## The Oil Embargo

Until 1973 King Faisal refrained from serious involvement in the Arab-Israeli confrontation—a conflict that had begun after the Jews established Israel as their national homeland in 1948. In 1973, however, the king assumed a prominent role in world politics after the outbreak of war between the State of Israel and the Arab states of Egypt and Syria.

King Saud spent millions of dollars constructing large palaces for his many wives and children. Nasriyah Gate is all that remains of the huge palace he built in Riyadh in 1956. King Faisal had most of this palace torn down because it highlighted the economic gulf between Saudi royalty and Saudi citizens.

Courtesy of U. S. Department of State

**31**

Faisal was under constant pressure from the leaders of other Arab states to use Saudi oil as a political weapon against Israel. These leaders called for an embargo, or halt, on Arab oil shipments to nations that supported Israel. Faisal agreed after the 1973 war began, and he reduced oil shipments to the West. When U.S. president Richard Nixon announced that he planned to increase the flow of arms to Israel, Faisal cut off all Saudi oil to the United States. Other Arab oil-producing nations and some members of OPEC also stopped shipments to the United States.

The embargo caused oil prices to rise from about $8 to $20 per barrel. It created an energy crisis among the industrial nations, some of whom, like Japan and the Western European countries, were heavily dependent on Arab oil. After U.S. secretary of state Henry Kissinger negotiated a cease-fire between Israel and its Arab opponents, the embargo came to an end in March 1974.

## Recent Events

In March 1975 King Faisal was assassinated by a young prince of the Saudi royal family. The assassin was later beheaded in public according to Saudi custom. Faisal's brother Khalid succeeded him to the throne.

Like Faisal, Khalid was a strong leader. He negotiated a border settlement in 1975 between Abu Dhabi (the largest region in the United Arab Emirates), Oman, and Saudi Arabia, and he worked to unify the Persian Gulf states. In addition, Khalid built industrial centers at Yanbu and Jubail, which allowed Saudi Arabia to refine its crude oil at home rather than overseas. Agricultural development, previously ignored by Saudi leaders, was another of Khalid's goals. Wheat production increased enormously during his reign.

Islamic extremists captured Mecca's large mosque, Al-Haram, in 1979, and this

Independent Picture Service

**King Faisal was the skilled leader of Saudi Arabia from 1964 to 1975. He reestablished the nation on a sound financial footing after the excesses of King Saud's monarchy.**

event rocked the Saud leadership. Rebels held the mosque for two weeks before they were removed at the cost of a number of lives. The incident was one of several outbreaks of domestic unrest and rioting that occurred in the late 1970s and early 1980s. In June 1982 King Khalid died, and he was succeeded by his half brother Crown Prince Fahd.

The new king responded to the increasing tensions of the Middle East region by expanding his diplomatic activity and by developing the nation's defense capability. Under King Fahd, Saudi Arabia bought sophisticated military equipment, mostly from the United States and Britain.

Another problem the king has faced is the falling value of oil. As a result of the oil surplus on the world market during the early 1980s, the Saudis have earned less money and have reduced spending in nearly every government department. Saudi leaders continue to work for satisfactory oil price levels and production quotas through OPEC.

Oil production continued to increase during King Khalid's reign (1975–1982).

Under King Khalid's leadership, agriculture, including the production of wheat in Asir, received special attention.

Jubail, a modern industrial city on the coast of the Persian Gulf, is one of King Khalid's most impressive accomplishments.

In addition to its internal concerns, Saudi Arabia continues to seek solutions to the region's tensions. In 1987, for example, Saudi Arabia reestablished relations with Egypt, which had been barred from the Arab League since 1979 when it signed a peace treaty with Israel.

In an effort to establish greater Arab unity, six nations of the Arabian Peninsula formed the Gulf Cooperation Council. The council called for resolution of the war between Iran and Iraq, which began in 1980. King Fahd and others urged Iran and Iraq to accept a cease-fire resolution proposed by the UN in 1987. After months of talks, which included appeals for peace by members of the council—including King Fahd—and by UN negotiators, Iran and Iraq agreed to a cease-fire in August 1988.

Courtesy of B. H. Moody/*Aramco World*

King Fahd – who came to power in 1982 when King Khalid unexpectedly died – is active in the search for solutions to the Middle East's difficulties.

Courtesy of U. S. Navy

A U.S. Navy ship *(left)* protects a supertanker *(right)* as it sails through the Persian Gulf. Both Iran and Iraq have attacked oil tankers in Saudi Arabian territorial waters and in the gulf.

A large, new housing complex in Riyadh accommodates only a small number of the people who have flocked to the city since the mid-twentieth century.

These six leaders represent their countries—Saudi Arabia, Kuwait, Bahrain, Qatar, Oman, and the United Arab Emirates—at a meeting of the Gulf Cooperation Council. One of the aims of the council is to increase the ability of member nations to defend themselves through shared information and joint military preparation.

## Government

Saudi Arabia is a monarchy, and the Koran serves as its constitution. The king, who is both chief of state and prime minister, exercises executive and legislative authority. A 25-member council of ministers is appointed by the king, and its responsibility is to advise him. The monarch also acts as the supreme religious leader of the country.

**35**

The government has planned and built modern, spacious cities to house the growing number of urban dwellers.

In the family-ruled house of Saud, power is held by male descendants of Ibn Saud, who founded the kingdom in 1932. The king consults with senior family members over policy matters until they reach consensus (general agreement). Ulama (religious scholars) and Western-educated

The national symbol of Saudi Arabia combines a date palm, which represents prosperity, and crossed swords, which stand for justice.

business and technical advisers hold minor consultative positions within the government. A crown prince, who will succeed the monarch, is named from among the sons of Ibn Saud in order to make the eventual transfer of kingship a peaceful one. The crown prince acts as the deputy prime minister.

The country functions within the framework of Arab tradition and Islamic law. The courts, whose magistrates are appointed by the Islamic leadership, are guided by the sharia, a collection of laws based on the Koran. The sharia consists of commentary and explanations of the basic points and rules set down in the Koran. The belief that criminals should suffer at least as much as their victims did determines the severity of punishment.

Political parties and elections do not exist in Saudi Arabia. Despite the rapid economic progress, the society remains conservative and religious. Although there is no representative government, a strong tradition of equality among males is present in Arab culture. Consequently, individuals have some rights, particularly the right to make complaints. The king and other royal ministers periodically hold majlis (audiences), which allow male Saudi subjects the opportunity to ask for help or to complain about difficult conditions. Female Saudis can make requests only through their husbands or male relatives.

The country is divided into 6 major and 12 minor provinces. Village leaders report to district governors and are responsible to them, assuring a certain amount of central control even in remote areas. Saudi Arabians often choose leaders based on family ties, and one family often dominates a village. Small local groups are headed by sheikhs, and when several groups band together, they form a major community whose most important sheikh (decided on the basis of social prestige) becomes the main leader.

Since becoming the king of Saudi Arabia in 1982, Fahd has brought the nation into a more prominent role of leadership among Middle Eastern countries.

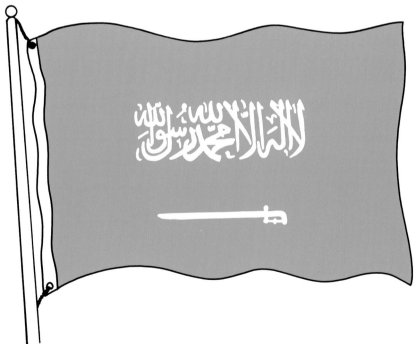

The Saudi Arabian flag is inscribed with the Islamic saying, "There is no God but Allah, and Muhammad is his Prophet." A sword lies beneath the inscription as a sign of the expansion of Islam through military conquests. The inscription and sword appear on a field of green – the color of Islam.

This finely woven Bedouin tapestry reflects the age-old skill of desert craftspeople.

Courtesy of Embassy of Kuwait

# 3) The People

A large proportion of Saudi Arabia's 14.2 million people once were nomads or seminomads, but recent economic growth has caused the country's settled population to increase steadily. In addition, the oil industry has attracted 1.5 million skilled and semiskilled workers—mostly Egyptians, Lebanese, and Palestinian Arabs—from other Arab countries, as well as people from Western nations. Drawn by the promise of good wages, nomadic and seminomadic Saudi Arabians have also moved into the cities.

## Nomadic and Village Life

About 10 percent of the population are Bedouin, an Arabic word that means "dwellers in the desert." The largest and most important Bedouin tribes in Saudi Arabia are the Ataiba, Har, Shammar, Mutair, and Dawasir. These peoples move in search of water and grazing lands for their herds of camels, sheep, or goats. The desert surrounding their pasturelands has limited Bedouin contact with other groups and cultures. As a result, their way of life has changed little through the centuries.

Bedouin traditionally live in cloth tents woven from goat or camel hair. Their social organization follows a set pattern—each tent represents a family, a group of families makes up a clan, and a number of clans constitute a tribe. Bedouin are fiercely loyal to members of their group, and they do not readily give loyalty to anyone else. Furthermore, they greatly value their honor and dignity. Consequently, an insult from the outside to any group member must be avenged. Generally the immediate family or the injured person deals with the offense. Continuing feuds over unresolved disputes may last for years, sometimes for generations.

In sharp contrast with the tradition of razzia, or raiding—which is now outlawed —is Bedouin hospitality. According to Bedouin custom, even a stranger must be given food, water, and shelter, because depriving a traveler of these essentials in the desert means certain death. For the first few days a guest is treated like a member of the family. Custom decrees that after a maximum of three days, the guest's special status expires.

The separation between nomadic Bedouin and settled farmers or villagers is not absolute. Bedouin depend on settled Arabs for food and tools, which they can obtain only by trading for these items. Also, farmers may become nomadic for the winter months, pasturing their animals in the desert, or they may entrust their animals to nomads to herd.

Villages are established near oases and grow only to the size that the available water supply can sustain. The oases often can support date plantations, fruit orchards, and some cereal (grain) crops. Ethnic groups gather in villages, living in areas separate from one another. Some groups have a wandering branch and a village branch, thus maintaining a nomadic as well as a settled lifestyle.

Saudis gather at the central market of Buraida in the 1950s. Buraida is a commercial city near Riyadh that started as a small oasis community. Dates were the main product of the settlement in the 1950s, and they continue to be an important crop in the region's economy.

Independent Picture Service

This enclosed courtyard represents the modern architectural styles used in Saudi Arabia's fast-developing urban areas.

## Urban Life

The 1960s and the 1970s were a time of tremendous development within Saudi Arabia's cities, which grew to hold over 70 percent of the population. Urban planners work to keep traditional Islamic features present in the architecture and organization of urban centers. No longer built of adobe, buildings are made of concrete, steel, and glass in the flowing, geometric designs common to Arab cultures. Residences are built around a central courtyard to give privacy to family members, especially to the women and young children. Courtyard walls also offer shade from the sun and protection from the often high winds. Extended families frequently cluster their homes together in walled-in compounds.

Due to the rapid migration of people to the cities, adequate urban housing is still one of the nation's main problems—despite the government's many building programs. The Ministry of Housing and Public Works built thousands of dwellings between 1980

Suqs offer items ranging from food to hardware and may be indoor markets or set up on open-air sites.

Architects have designed modern homes to include elements of traditional Arabic design. For example, the white color of the house reflects most of the sun's rays, thereby retaining less heat, and the narrow windows limit the amount of heat-producing sunlight that enters the dwelling.

With large numbers of people moving to the cities, many more units of housing have been built to accommodate new urban residents. The roof of each home in this development has solar panels, which transform solar energy into electricity.

and 1985. In recent years, private construction firms also have been active in helping to meet Saudi housing needs. The government is trying to provide living quarters for low- and middle-income groups.

The growing urban areas are a focus for change in Saudi Arabian society. No longer strictly separated into residential sections according to clan, groups new to Saudi social organization now live in the cities. Students, government workers, and technicians are altering the traditional social patterns because these newcomers do not live in locations that are restricted to clans or extended families.

Pilgrims (religious travelers) visit the hill on the plain of Arafat where Muhammad spoke his last sermon.

Courtesy of S. M. Amin/*Aramco World*

## Religion

Religion has been the single most important element in the history of Arabia. The birth of Islam in the seventh century A.D. united the inhabitants of the Arabian Peninsula for the first time, giving them a common identity.

Islam rests on five duties: declaring faith, praying five times daily, giving to the poor, fasting, and making a pilgrimage to Mecca once in a lifetime. Nearly all Saudi Arabians are Sunni Muslims (a sect of Islam that accepts Islamic leaders who do not descend from Muhammad's family). Most belong to the strict Wahhabi subgroup, which practices a variation of Sunni doctrine. About 10 percent are Shiites (those who follow only the leaders descended from Muhammad's family), and most Shiites live in the Al-Hasa region.

Religious freedom exists in other Muslim countries, but Saudi Arabia only permits Islam. The practice of any other religion is strictly forbidden, except for noncitizens such as oil company employees and businesspeople.

The Koran—considered the summary of the revelations by Allah to Muhammad—consists of 114 suras (chapters), which are

Courtesy of *Aramco World*

A young Saudi boy, dressed in ceremonial clothing, reads an elaborately decorated copy of the Koran.

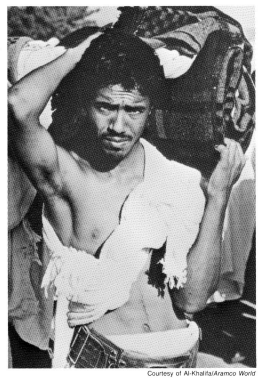

With his bedroll on his shoulder, this pilgrim wears the traditional white garments of the Islamic hajj (religious journey or pilgrimage).

written in classical Arabic, and the book is the main link among the world's 800 million Muslims.

One of the most important parts of Islam is the hajj, or pilgrimage, to Mecca. Muslims from many countries gather each year to make this sacred journey. During the pilgrimage, all social and political differences among travelers are temporarily ignored. Every pilgrim, whether rich or poor, wears the same simple white garment and participates in the same rituals. Some arrive in Mecca in air-conditioned cars, while others are crowded into huge trucks or buses, and still others come on foot.

Once in Mecca, the pilgrim stops at the Kaaba, a large cube-shaped structure in the center of Al-Haram. The Kaaba is covered with heavy, dark curtains embroidered with verses from the Koran. Each Muslim circles the structure seven times. Those who are sick or disabled are carried around it on stretchers. Muslims all over the world turn toward the Kaaba five times each day to pray.

During the hajj, the central courtyard of Al-Haram is packed with visitors surrounding the Kaaba.

Many new housing areas, such as this one in Jubail, are equipped with playgrounds for children.

## Education and Language

In the past many Saudi Arabians, particularly the Bedouin and those who lived in small villages, never saw a book other than the Koran. With the increase of wealth from the oil industry, the educational system grew quickly in the 1970s.

In the late 1980s schooling was free in Saudi Arabia and was provided on three levels—elementary, intermediate, and secondary. Commercial, agricultural, and vocational schools offer specialized training programs.

Women account for about 30 percent of the students—a figure that represents an increase of 18 percent since 1960. Boys and girls attend separate schools, even at the university level. Adults without previous education may enroll in a four-year night-school course to study for an elementary educational certificate. The first two years of school are devoted entirely to learning to read and write, in an attempt to improve the nation's literacy rate of 48 percent.

King Saud University, founded in 1950, has a $2-billion campus designed to accommodate 22,000 students. In addition to eight main buildings and a library, the complex has a mosque and a teaching hospital for medical students. The university offers degrees in medicine, engineering, science, commerce, agriculture, dentistry, history, mass media, and sociology. King Abdul Aziz University, with campuses in Jidda and Mecca, was founded in 1967. The University of Petroleum and Minerals

Young Saudis study in a resource room at an elementary school for boys.

Students walk through the huge hall that leads to the library at King Saud University. Most students wear traditional clothing; only a few attend classes in Western-style dress.

Courtesy of Jill Hartley/*Aramco World*

Courtesy of Royal Commission of Jubail and Yanbu

Schools at every level are well equipped with modern educational technology. Here, Saudi Arabian students use computers that display Arabic script on their monitors.

Arabic letters are formed in different styles for different occasions. Thickly drawn characters *(top row)* are for everyday use, while a more ornamental form *(middle row)* is used for special occasions. The most ornate style of lettering *(bottom row)* appears primarily in headlines and titles.

Independent Picture Service

opened in Dhahran in 1963 and is a leading technical institution with students from over 50 nations.

English is taught throughout the country, but Arabic—a Semitic tongue related to Hebrew and Aramaic—is the language of instruction. Although Arabic has many local dialects, people from different parts of the country can still understand each other. The written language uses flowing, rounded, and connected characters that are read from right to left.

## Health

Saudi Arabia's chief health problems are typical of those found in many developing countries. Malnutrition was once widespread and caused anemia (a blood disease), scurvy (a disease of the teeth and gums), and tuberculosis. Stomach ailments, trachoma (an eye disease often causing blindness), and typhoid were also common. Since 1950, however, impressive improvements in health standards have taken place.

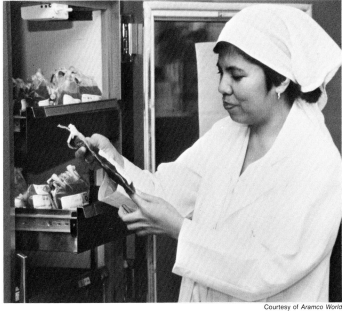

Courtesy of *Aramco World*

A health-care worker checks on the blood supply in a laboratory of King Fahd Hospital. The Saudi Arabian government has invested heavily in establishing a high-quality health-care system for the nation.

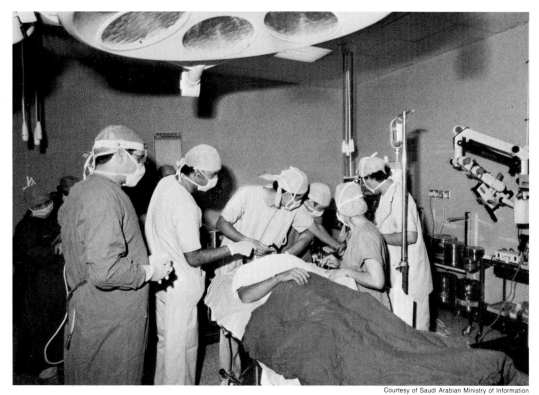

Saudi Arabia's medical centers are equipped with the finest technology and are staffed by well-trained personnel.

A long-standing health problem has resulted from the yearly migration of religious pilgrims to Mecca. These travelers frequently carry a variety of contagious (catchable) diseases. The government has planned new health-care facilities to serve both Saudi citizens and the pilgrims. In 1987, 55 government hospitals, 600 clinics, and 350 health units were in operation. Twenty-three mobile units regularly tour the remote parts of the country. Nearly 50 private hospitals and clinics are open, and additional hospitals are under construction.

Strict laws have now been enacted to curb contagious diseases. Medical workers offer immunization throughout the country, and special mobile teams regularly inspect water and sewer systems. About 93 percent of the population have access to safe drinking water. Various UN agencies have helped to establish medical facilities that pay special attention to preventive medicine.

Despite these governmental efforts, infant mortality remains high, at about 85 deaths in the first year per 1,000 live births, although this figure is average for the region. The life expectancy—61 years of age—is also average among Middle Eastern countries. Health-care facilities are undergoing huge expansion, and the government intends to provide free, comprehensive medical care. In 1985 about 90 percent of Saudi Arabia's medical personnel were from foreign countries. The government is trying to encourage more Saudis, especially women, to enter the health-care field.

## The Arts and Communications

According to a strict interpretation of the Koran, music is not allowed in religious

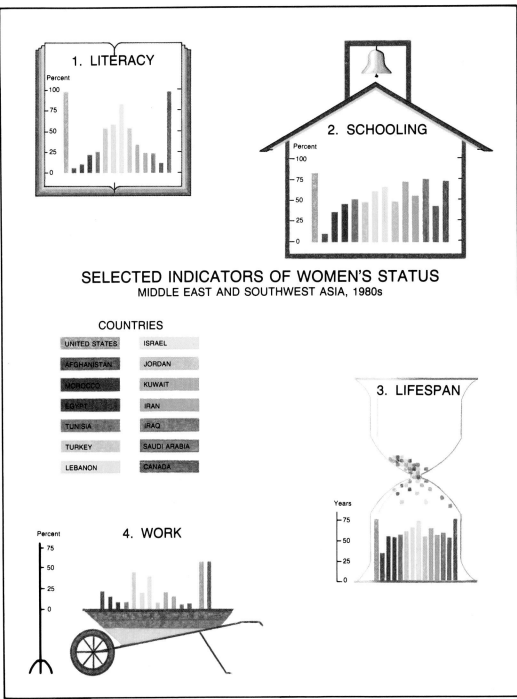

Artwork by Carol F. Barrett

Depicted in this chart are factors relating to the status of women in the Middle East and southwest Asia. Graph 1, labeled Literacy, shows the percentage of adult women who can read and write. Graph 2 illustrates the proportion of school-aged girls who actually attend elementary and secondary schools. Graph 3 depicts the life expectancy of female babies at birth. Graph 4 shows the percentage of women in the income-producing work force. Data taken from *Women in the World: An International Atlas,* 1986 and from *Women . . . A World Survey,* 1985.

services, and often it does not have a place in private life. But the Bedouin have developed a distinctive chant accompanied by a rebab (a one-stringed instrument) and drums, and increasingly more music is heard in Saudi society, primarily as a result of the influence of radio and television. The newer music is a mixture of traditional and modern styles that are borrowed from other Arabic countries.

Visual arts used to be almost unknown in Saudi Arabia. The Koran is often interpreted to have a strict rule against pictures —including paintings and photographs— so there is very little painting, photography, or sculpture in the country. The visual arts have found an outlet in the making of hand-lettered and illustrated Korans and in the striking Arabic architecture that is based on geometric designs.

In pre-Islamic Arabia, poetry and other forms of literature were widespread. After Muhammad and the coming of Islam in the seventh century, poetic expression declined, because Muhammad did not approve of the romantic verse that was common at the time. The older literature of Arabia is full of stories and poems celebrating romantic love, heroes, war, and the beauty and intelligence of Arabian horses and camels. Poetry and storytelling have been instrumental in preserving Saudi Arabia's history and culture.

Television and radio are popular sources of entertainment. Television shows are varied, consisting of educational broadcasts, readings from the Koran, and entertainment programs produced in Egypt. The voice of a Saudi woman was heard for the first time on the radio in 1963, and since then women have played a more prominent role in the media.

Eight daily newspapers are published, and nine other newspapers appear periodically. Magazines range from popular publications to literary and scientific reviews. Most of the journals are privately owned but are supported by government advertising and special tax privileges. The

Courtesy of Katrina Thomas/*Aramco World*

A craftsperson traces the embroidery pattern for this cloth, which has verses from the Koran sewn into the fabric. Artists in this workshop in Mecca use gold and silver threads to make religious tapestries that are hung in Islamic holy places.

government is aware of the activities of the press, and, although there is no direct censorship, newspapers are expected not to publish anything offensive to the state.

## Marriage, Social Life, and Customs

Although the Koran permits a man to have four wives—if they are treated equally—most Saudi Arabian men have only one marriage partner. Marriages usually occur between distant relatives and are arranged by the parents. Often the young couple see each other for the first time during the wedding ceremony. Before the marriage is agreed upon, a dowry must be paid to the bride's family by either the groom or his family. Some Western-educated young people in Saudi Arabia are breaking with these traditions and are choosing their own marriage partners.

A man can easily divorce his wife, by saying on three occasions, "you are divorced from me." He has certain obligations, however, such as providing for the couple's children. It is much more difficult for a woman to obtain a divorce. Although

A group of Saudis gathers for conversation, music, and coffee. The musician *(center)* plays a rebab, a one-stringed instrument of Bedouin origin.

the Koran has many references to the rights and fair treatment of women, they have a less visible and less influential position in traditional Arab society than men do.

Men and women very rarely socialize together—even when close families gather. Saudi women are required to wear veils in public and in the presence of strangers. Generally, women are not welcome in the country's business and political life, but in recent years women have gradually become involved in the medical field and in some social and charitable activities. Public activities in which both sexes participate are almost nonexistent. While men often gather in coffee shops to smoke, gossip, and drink coffee, women do not freely meet outside the home.

## Food and Recreation

A customary meal in Saudi Arabia consists of mutton that is served on a large platter with rice, roasted or fried eggplant, salad, eggs, and cheese. Dessert often includes fruit or a custardlike mixture with raisins or almonds. The bread eaten with the meal is soft, flat, and round and is

A Bedouin tends coffee beans as they roast over a fire. Constant stirring helps the beans brown evenly, after which they are pounded into a fine powder and sweetened with spices. The coffee is served from small metal pots.

Courtesy of M. S. Al-Shabeeb/*Aramco World*

**Sports in Saudi Arabia range from traditional camel races** *(above)* **to the newly introduced game of soccer** *(below).*

often large and thin enough to be folded over several times.

Because Islam strictly forbids the consumption of alcoholic beverages, they are unavailable in Saudi Arabia. Even visitors or foreigners working in the country are not allowed to buy liquor. In Arabia, coffee drinking is a social institution, and whenever Arabs get together, coffee is served. To prepare Arabian coffee, the beans are roasted in small quantities, pounded very fine, mixed with sugar and water, and then simmered in coffee pots. The result is a sweet beverage, scented with cardamom, a gingerlike spice.

Camel and horse racing and hunting with dogs or falcons (hawks) are the favorite traditional sports of Saudi Arabia. Falconry continues among the wealthy. Most falcons are brought from Iraq and Iran. These birds are trained to hunt other birds and small animals.

Since 1950 Saudi Arabians have begun to take up Western sports. Basketball and soccer are particularly popular in the cities and at the oil installations. Exercise programs and gymnastics are now part of physical education courses in schools. More than 700 athletic clubs offer activities varying from soccer to swimming and from track and field to table tennis. Several modern stadiums have been built. The most impressive sports facility lies in the capital city of Riyadh.

Courtesy of David Luttrell/*Aramco World*

Miles of pipe await assembly into lines that will carry oil from drilling areas to refining facilities.

Courtesy of Mobil Oil Corporation

# 4) The Economy

The greatest single factor of economic importance in Saudi Arabia is the abundant presence of oil. Production is constantly increasing, and in the mid-1980s the country was producing 23.4 billion barrels per year. As a result of its oil sales, Saudi Arabia has a per capita (per person) income comparable to that of wealthier Western nations.

## The Oil Industry

The discovery of oil and the development of the petroleum industry by ARAMCO created the need for new roads, jobs, airports, and housing. When ARAMCO engineers came to Saudi Arabia, they explored and mapped much of the country for the first time.

Oil revenues increased slowly in the 1950s and 1960s, and the country did not become one of the world's major producers and exporters until the 1970s. With a rise in oil prices Saudi Arabia's oil income skyrocketed from $4.3 billion in 1973 to $22.6 billion in 1974. The huge sales enabled the Saudi Arabian government to buy 25 percent of U.S.-owned ARAMCO, and in 1979 the Saudi government negotiated with ARAMCO's owners to take full control of the firm. By 1981 oil revenues had reached nearly $102 billion.

An oil rig drills in the Ghawar oil field—the largest known oil site yet discovered, as of the late 1980s.

Saudi Arabia has rich deposits of oil beneath its territorial waters. Specially built offshore drilling rigs extract the valuable resource.

The crude petroleum that is pumped from the ground must be refined before it can be used. This facility in Jidda removes impurities from the oil, processing it into gasoline or other petroleum-based products.

This pipeline carries oil from underground fields to a refinery in the city of Yanbu on the Red Sea—a distance of 750 miles.

In the early 1980s, however, a surplus of oil on the world market reduced the nation's revenues. Because Saudi Arabia depended on oil for more than 97 percent of its income, the low demand for Saudi oil led to a drop of 18 percent in the nation's gross domestic product (GDP, the total amount of goods and services produced within the country in a year). By 1986 Saudi Arabia's GDP had recovered to $98 billion.

Saudi Arabia has proven oil reserves of 169 billion barrels—or about 25 percent of the world's total. The known amount of reserves increases each year as more oil is discovered. By using money from oil sales, the Saudi government has expanded its processing capability and has developed refining and marketing facilities. With the help of several international firms, ARAMCO, the country's primary oil producer, is searching for oil in the central part of the country—an area that so far has remained largely unexplored.

Although tankers ship Saudi oil to Europe and Japan to be refined, Saudis are refining increasing amounts in their own country. Until 1960 the refinery at Ras Tanura was Saudi Arabia's only processing facility. In 1987 two newer refineries with advanced technology were operating at Jubail and Yanbu. These facilities produced over 800,000 barrels per day of refined products, including gasoline and kerosene.

Some oil is carried by pipelines to the island of Bahrain. Natural gas, a by-product of crude oil deposits, was once considered a useless nuisance. Now, however, the gas is collected to use as fuel and is piped to purification plants in Al-Hasa. In the 1980s ARAMCO produced 156 million barrels of natural gas liquids that resulted from crude oil production.

## Agriculture and Industry

Agriculture is limited to the Asir region and to oases that have adequate rainfall or sufficient well water. Some areas of Nejd and Al-Hasa are being developed, but less than 1 percent of Saudi Arabian land is used for farming. The prices of Saudi agricultural goods are high compared with average world markets because the water needed to irrigate the land is very expensive to obtain.

Farm workers weed a field of squash at an agricultural research station in the Asir region of southwestern Saudi Arabia. A small dam regulates the flow that irrigates the crops.

A pipe irrigation system waters a field of maize (corn). Finding an efficient means of using the nation's limited water supply is the biggest problem Saudi farmers face.

Courtesy of Saudi Arabian Ministry of Information

Desalinization installations that turn salt water into usable liquid have made possible many new irrigation projects, like this sprinkler-watered wheat field.

The Saudi government is working to extend the country's agricultural potential by funding programs to turn the desert into farmland. This process involves irrigation, proper drainage, and control of surface water and blowing sand. Government funds are used to construct dams, to purify water for drinking, and to establish centers that offer technical assistance to farmers.

Dates, an important food crop, are one of the mainstays of the Saudi diet. This dependency on dates is changing, however, as Saudi farmers begin to grow a wider variety of vegetables, fruits, and grains. Especially striking has been the increase in the production of cereal grains. In 1977 wheat production totaled 300,000 tons, but by 1985 this figure had risen to 1.3 million tons—giving a yearly harvest that supplied almost all of the wheat consumed in the kingdom. Other leading crops are

Courtesy of Saudi Arabian Ministry of Information

At Najran, an automated factory bottles the spring water taken from underground sources.

By clinging to the trunk, a worker gathers clusters of fruit from the top of a date palm tree.

alfalfa, watermelons, and citrus products. Livestock estimates include 3.5 million sheep, 2.3 million goats, 500,000 cattle, 160,000 camels, and 110,000 donkeys.

Saudi Arabia's industrial goods—outside of oil—include cement, plastics, soap, shoes, clothing, and other consumer items.

The country still relies heavily on imported goods, foodstuffs, and machinery. Saudi Arabia's major trading partners are the United States, Great Britain, Japan, West Germany, and Italy. Industries unrelated to petroleum combine to contribute only 2 percent to the GDP.

Jidda, Saudi Arabia's main port on the Red Sea, has been considerably expanded and modernized in the 1980s.

## Transportation

Saudi Arabia's main ports are Jidda, Dammam, Yanbu, and Jizan. Port facilities are expanding to accommodate the increasing flow of exports and imports. Ras Tanura historically was the most important oil-loading port, serving thousands of tankers yearly. On the Arabian coast large numbers of traditional Arab sailing ships, called dhows, are anchored alongside large oceangoing vessels. Built by hand of the finest hardwoods and soaked with shark oil, the dhows still carry small cargoes along the coasts.

Diesel trucks have replaced camels as Saudi Arabia's main means of transportation, although donkeys are still often used in the distant settled areas. About 16,000 miles of paved roads carry motor traffic. In 1967 the government built a 950-mile asphalt road connecting Dammam on the Persian Gulf with Riyadh and the Red Sea port of Jidda. Recently a six-lane highway linking Mecca and Medina was opened. A 15-mile-long causeway (a highway over water) links Saudi Arabia and Bahrain.

Saudi Arabia has a large fleet of commercial aircraft, including 80 planes that fly to 38 foreign countries. The main airports at Jidda, Dhahran, and Riyadh handle large, modern jets. The Saudi Arabian government built a huge airport near Jidda. Opened in 1982, the airport covers an area of 41 square miles and has 123 airfields. The site was designed by French engineers who modeled it after Charles de Gaulle Airport in Paris. Other smaller airports form an important link in the country's growing transportation network. Saudia, the government-owned airline, flies to North Africa, to most European destinations, and to some Asian cities.

Courtesy of Royal Commission of Jubail and Yanbu

The service harbor of King Fahd Port at Yanbu contains a fleet of tugs and pilot boats that guide large ships in and out of the docks.

Courtesy of Saudi Arabian Ministry of Information

A Saudia jet takes on passengers at King Khalid International Airport in Riyadh.

Courtesy of Saudi Arabian Ministry of Information

The Saudi Public Transport Company operates buses throughout the nation but particularly focuses its services around Mecca and Medina during the time of the annual Muslim pilgrimage.

This station handles regional demands for electricity, which increased by over 30 percent during the early 1980s.

The nation has engaged in a variety of water projects—including processing seawater into a usable form and taking better advantage of underground resources. Through these efforts the Saudis hope to satisfy the growing demand for water from the industrial, agricultural, and residential sectors.

## Water and Energy

One of the greatest problems in Saudi Arabia is its lack of water. Very little land in the country is suitable for farming, and the government has built several small dams to conserve water, as well as a large dam at the city of Abha in the south.

A huge water-desalting plant (a facility that removes salt from seawater) operates near Jidda and has a daily processing capacity of five million gallons. Thirteen other plants have been opened, and another 12 are planned. Because desalinization is very expensive, however, it cannot meet all the water needs of the population.

Electric plants generate over 17 billion kilowatt-hours of energy per year, mostly for use in the major cities. Many small settlements have their own electrical plants. All of the generating plants are powered by diesel engines, which allow Saudi Arabia to use its vast oil resources to produce electric power. In addition, Saudis use the nation's petroleum products to power their growing number of automobiles.

Courtesy of Saudi Arabian Ministry of Information

Tall towers support power lines as they pass over some of the rough terrain of the Hejaz region. Diesel turbines generate the electricity that is carried to settlements throughout the area.

Courtesy of Royal Commission of Jubail and Yanbu

A Saudi technician monitors purity levels at a plant that removes salt from seawater.

## The Future

Several difficulties weigh upon Saudi Arabia as it enters the 1990s. Since 1980 the war between Iran and Iraq, two of Saudi Arabia's Persian Gulf neighbors, has created political strife. As they sail through the gulf, many oil tankers—including some that belong to Saudi Arabia—have been attacked by both Iran and Iraq. In addition, the 1987 clash between Saudi armed forces and Iranians making their pilgrimage to Mecca left several hundred people dead and greatly increased the tensions between the two countries. As a result, Saudi Arabia is dramatically increasing its defense budget in an effort to prepare for possible future confrontations in the region.

Another difficulty stems from the drop in oil prices. From a high in 1981 of $34 per barrel, the oil price fell to a low of $10 per barrel and stabilized in 1987 at $18 per barrel. This loss of profits has prevented Saudi Arabia from carrying out some of its development plans. The government has not, however, cut back on the

Courtesy of *Aramco World*

Well Number Seven was Saudi Arabia's first productive oil well. Even though ARAMCO's leases of territory were established in 1933, it was not until 1938 that a successful well was drilled. Active until 1982, Well Number Seven now has a gleaming coat of aluminum paint and stands as a reminder of the development fostered by the nation's oil industry.

Courtesy of *Aramco World*

Portable housing placed over sections of pipeline protects workers from the desert sun. Saudi Arabia continues to develop its oil resources and to use the profits from this industry to enrich other aspects of its national life.

Saudi Arabia's oil wealth will continue to provide educational opportunities and medical care for the nation's youth through government-supported programs.

free educational or medical services it offers to its people, nor has it ended its program of housing loans.

Saudi Arabia continues to make use of its oil profits for the growth of a strong Arab and Islamic nation. The ruling monarchs are careful not to allow modernization to overcome the nation's religious orientation. Amid many tensions from both inside and outside the country, Saudi Arabia remains the keeper of Islam's holy places and the spiritual center of the world's 555 million Muslims.

Each year Saudi Arabia is host to the world's Muslim pilgrims, providing temporary tent housing and maintaining transportation routes for the millions who visit the nation's Islamic holy places.

**63**

# Index

Abd al-Aziz al-Saud. *See* Ibn Saud
Abha, 60
Abu Dhabi, 32
Afghanistan, 27
Africa, 24–25, 27
Agriculture, 4, 10, 13, 21, 32, 54–57. *See also* Dates; Livestock; Wheat
Air transportation, 31, 58–59
Arab League, 7, 34
Arabia, 24–29
Arabian American Oil Company (ARAMCO), 22, 31, 52, 54
Arabian Peninsula, 7, 9, 15–16, 23–24, 27, 34, 42
Arabian Sea, 24
Arabic, 23, 26, 42–43, 46
Arab-Israeli conflict, 31–32
Archaeology, 23
Architecture, 19, 40–41, 49
Arts, 47, 49
Asia, 27
Asir, 9–11, 14, 54–55
Bahrain, 35, 54, 58
Bedouin, 38–39, 44, 47, 49
Boundaries, 9
Buraida, 39
Camels, 12, 15, 25, 51, 58
Cities, 18–22, 36. *See also* Buraida; Dhahran; Jidda; Jubail; Mecca; Medina; Riyadh; Yanbu
Climate, 7, 13–14
Clothing, 42–43, 50
Coffee, 50–51
Communications, 49, 60
Customs, 49–50
Dammam, 18, 58
Dates, 13, 21, 39, 56–57
Desert, 7, 11–13, 25
Dhahran, 22–23, 46, 58
Dilmun (civilization), 24
Domestic unrest, 32–33, 62–63
Economy, 8, 30, 52–63
Education, 44–46, 48
Egypt, 24, 27–28, 31, 34
Egrets, 15
Electricity, 60–61
Energy, 16, 60–61
Ethnic groups, 22, 38–39
Europe, 32, 54
Exports, 30–33, 52, 54, 57–58, 62–63
Fahd, King, 8, 32, 34, 37
Faisal, 31–32
Fauna, 14–16
Fertile Crescent, 24
Fish, 15
Flag, 37
Flora, 14–15
Food, 50–51
Future outlook, 8, 62–63
Germany, 29, 57
Government, 35–37, 56, 62–63
Grains, 21, 33, 39, 56
Great Britain, 29, 57
Gulf Cooperation Council, 34–35
Al-Haram (grand mosque), 8, 19, 20, 32, 43
Al-Hasa, 9, 11–12, 22, 29, 42, 54

Health, 46–47
Hejaz, 9–11, 13, 15, 20, 22, 27–28, 31
History, 23–34
    ancient history, 23–25
    birth of Islam, 26–27
    current, 32–34
    impact of oil, 30–34
    Kingdom of Saudi Arabia, 29–34
    Saud dynasty, 28–34
Horses, 15, 51
House of Saud, 36
Housing, 39–41, 63
Hussein, Emir, 29
Ibn Saud, 29, 36
Imports, 57–58
India, 24–25, 27
Industry, 7–8, 17–18, 30–33, 52–54, 57, 63
Iran, 8, 16, 34, 62
Iraq, 8–9, 24, 27, 34, 62
Irrigation, 13, 54–56
Islam, 4, 8, 20–21, 26–29, 32–33, 36, 42–43, 49, 63
Islamic University, 21
Israel, 24, 31–32, 34
Italy, 57
Japan, 32, 54, 57
Jidda, 22, 25, 45, 53, 57–58, 60, 63
Jizan, 58
Jordan, 9, 25
Jubail, 32–33, 44, 54
Judicial system, 36–37
Khalid, King, 32–33
King Abdul Aziz University, 45
King Fahd Port, 58
King Saud University, 44–45
Kissinger, Henry, 32
Koran, 21, 26, 28, 35–36, 42–43, 47, 49
Kuwait, 9, 16, 35
Labor force, 38
Land, 9–22
Language, 23, 44, 46
Lawrence of Arabia, 29
Literacy, 44, 48
Literature, 49
Livestock, 13, 38, 57
Locusts, 15
Manufacturing, 17–18, 57
Maps and charts, 6, 10, 24, 48
Markets, 21–22, 40
Marriage, 49–50
Al-Masane, 17
Mecca, 4, 10, 18–22, 25–28, 32, 42–43, 47, 58, 62
Medina, 21, 25–26, 58
Medina Library, 21
Mediterranean Sea, 24
Middle East, 7, 29, 33, 47, 60
Mining, 17
Minerals, 16–17
Mosques, 8, 20
Muhammad, 19, 26–27, 42, 49
Murraba Palace, 34
Music, 47, 49–50
Muslims, 4, 8, 20–22, 26–29, 36, 38, 42–43, 63
Nabataeans, 23, 25

Al-Nafud, 9, 11
Najran, 56
Natural resources, 16–17
Nejd, 9, 11, 18, 27–29, 54
Nixon, President Richard, 32
Nomads, 23–24, 38–39
Oases, 10–13, 18, 21, 39, 54
Oil, 7–8, 11–12, 16–17, 22, 31–34, 52–54, 58, 62–63
Oil embargo, 31–32
Oman, 9, 32, 35
Organization of Petroleum Exporting Countries (OPEC), 8, 32
Ottoman Empire, 28–29
People, 38–51
People's Democratic Republic of Yemen, 9
Persian Gulf, 8–9, 11, 13, 16, 18, 23–24, 34, 62
Persians, 25
Petroleum, 7–8, 11, 16–17, 30–34, 52–54, 58, 60
Pilgrimages, 20–22, 38, 43, 47, 62
Political parties, 36
Population, 18, 21, 38
Ports, 22, 57–58
Portugal, 28
Qatar, 9, 35
Quraysh (tribe), 25
Rainfall, 7, 11, 13–14
Ras Tanura, 54, 58
Red Sea, 9, 13, 15, 22, 28
Refineries, 30, 32–33, 52–54
Religion, 4, 20–22, 26–27, 35–37, 42–43, 63
Riyadh, 13, 17–19, 29, 35, 51, 58–59
Roads and highways, 58
Rub al-Khali (Empty Quarter), 7, 9, 11, 14, 16
Sabaeans, 25
King Saud ibn Abd al-Aziz, 31
Saudi Arabia,
    boundaries, size, and location of, 9
    flag of, 37
    future outlook of, 8, 62–63
    population of, 38
Saudi Public Transport Company, 59
Saudia (airline), 59
Sauds, 28–29, 31–32
Shiite Muslims, 42
Sinai Peninsula, 24
Social life, 49–50
Solar energy, 17
Sports and recreation, 5, 50–51
Sunni Muslims, 42
Syria, 24, 27–28, 31, 34
Topography, 9–12
Trade, 24–25
Transportation, 31, 58–59
Tuwayq, Jebel, 11
Umayyad, 27
United Arab Emirates, 9, 32, 35
United Nations (UN), 8, 34, 47
United States, 31–32, 34, 57
Universities, 45–46

University of Petroleum and Minerals, 45
Urban life, 8, 18–19, 40–41, 63
Venezuela, 7–8
Village life, 37–39
Wahhabis, 42
Wahhabism, 28
Water supply, 13, 54–56, 60
Well Number Seven, 62
Women, 44, 47–50
World War I, 29
Yanbu, 14, 32, 54, 58
Yemen Arab Republic, 9